# THE TECHNIQUE CATASTROPHE

## An Explanation of the Multitudes of False Professions in the Independent Baptist Movement.

by

**Bob Creel**

Printed in the United States of America

Republished with permission from Pastor Bob Creel
By
The Old Paths Publications
2021

REL: Religion with Interpretation

**ISBN: 978-1-7356723-9-7**

All Scripture quotations are from the King James Bible.



Address All Inquiries To:
THE OLD PATHS PUBLICATIONS, Inc.
142 Gold Flume Way
Cleveland, Georgia, U.S.A.

Web: www.theoldpathspublications.com
E-mail: TOP@theoldpathspublications.com

# FORWARD

Through the pages of this book, I embark on a project that I have avoided for a number of years. Part of me says that it is because I have lacked the time for such an undertaking, while the rest of me admits to the fact that even as King Saul of old, "...**I feared the people**..." (1 Samuel 15:24), when associated with the contents of this book. Sometimes, striving for the acceptance of "the brethren" causes us to keep silent when something needs to be said.

It finally occurred to me that though there would be multitudes of brethren that would agree with some of the things that I am about to say, they wouldn't say it themselves for fear of losing their place in "The Pecking Order." Because I have no position in anyone's pecking order, I probably stand to lose the least when commenting on such a "sacred cow" as Independent Baptists' soul-winning practices.

I remember a discussion that I had with a pastor friend of mine several years ago about this very subject. My father lived in his area and when visiting him, this good brother would always have me preach in his church. Usually, when this pastor brother and I got together, the first thing that he wanted to talk about was the number of people that were led to Christ through our ministries. The first year he was elated to inform me that he led 800 people to Christ during that particular calendar year. When he asked me how many I had led to Christ at the church where I was pastoring, I rather sheepishly estimated that it was probably about 15 or 20, though we don't keep records of those who we felt we had won to the Lord.

After five consecutive years of this same scenario, I noticed that the attendance of his church didn't seem to be changing much. Although he seemed to be stuck around the same number that was introduced to Christ that year, and my estimates for the church that I pastored was usually in the same ballpark, there was a drastic difference in our attendance! That five-year period had produced approximately 4,000 souls through his soul-winning endeavors, while the same time frame yielded about 100 for me. Noticing the imbalance in his figures in relation to his attendance increase, I asked him what his Sunday morning attendance average was five years ago, and what it was currently. His reply was 98 then and about 110 now. I informed him that my church attendance was about 50 then and over 300 now. Trying to keep a straight face, I then asked him if it didn't seem strange to him that while he was running circles around me in-so-far as "leading people to Christ," his church attendance only increased about 10%, while mine more than quadrupled during the same time frame!

This story can only be surpassed with the account of a revival service that I had in my last pastorate. Carefully choosing what I was led to believe was a successful nationally-known evangelist, I scheduled a week's revival. During my 12 years as pastor, this was undoubtedly the worst meetings that I ever had! He turned out to be one of those fellows who made a lot of noise but didn't say anything. The attendance each evening grew worse. By Thursday night he informed me that he overlooked the fact that he had double-booked for Friday night and couldn't finish out our meetings but would leave his assistant to close out the last night. I declined and preached Friday night myself. I somehow got the feeling that if the crowd was up, and the offering would have also been up, there probably wouldn't have been a "double-booking" problem.

Shortly thereafter, I was reading the accounts of meetings by evangelists in one of our Baptist periodicals, when I came across this brother's name. I was curious as to whether-or-not some of the other brethren were having better results with this evangelist than I experienced, so I began to read the report of his meetings. As I read along, I was surprised to see his account of heaven coming down, the altars being full, and 8 souls being saved at this particular meeting. Finishing the account only increased my surprise when I read that the meeting was at my church! That sounded a far cry from the altars being empty, the crowd decreasing each evening, no one getting saved, and heaven flying its flag half-mast by Thursday!

When numbers become so important to us that they outweigh the truth – it's time that we admit to a crisis! When we receive missionary reports similar to the one recently sent to the church where I am now attending, it's time we take stock of our methodology. This missionary brother was rejoicing over the results that he had experienced in his first full year on the field, after taking this existing work. He boasted of 738 professions of faith with 25 following in believer's baptism. How could you even pen those words without asking yourself if there isn't something wrong with that picture? I seem to remember 3,000 saved at Pentecost – and 3,000 baptized!

My wife arrived home one afternoon many years ago, after spending her weekly appointed time with a ladys' soul-winning group. Excited about the day's results, she informed me that she led 80 souls to Christ that day. I probably would have shared her excitement had she not gone into detail of the day's happenings. It seems as though they had her put on a snowman's suit to pass out candy in one of the local parks. Each time that she could get a small group of children together, she told them the story of Jesus and had them to repeat a prayer after her. They were then declared saved and given the assurance of their salvation. For those of you who are wondering, after studying the Bible on these issues, my wife repented of the foolishness that she was taught, and exchanged man's teachings for Biblical principles on the subject of witnessing.

I hope that you have noted thus far that I have not cited any institutions, clubs, or organizations in the forward of this book, not will I in the body of its content. It is not my intent to sling mud, grind axes, or expose anyone who is involved in this "technique catastrophe," but rather to arrive at a position of sanity and truth in regards to the witnessing of our faith. When teaching some of the content of this book in a church in Wisconsin, a dear layman summed up my concern when he said with tears in his eyes, "Don't people understand that we are messing with someone's forever?"

Perhaps as Hilkiah of old, it becomes our duty not only to clean out those things from the house of God that displease Him, but also to find The Book of God and discover once again what His teachings are on some of these subjects! You will note throughout this book that our intent is to draw to your attention how much our witnessing and soul-winning technique has no bearing nor teaching from His Book, but rather from man's tradition. God being my helper, my intent is to follow up on this book with one entitled, "Fruit in Your Basket."* Because we have strayed so far from what the Bible teaches on this subject, I felt it necessary to begin this project with the "how-not-tos."

The burden of this book is not to produce an apologetic that proves that I am right and you are wrong, but rather for you to muse on the fact that if you are wrong, you are not only producing false professions – you could be indeed pushing people into hell! Remember, you are messing with someone's "forever"!

# TABLE OF CONTENTS

# CHAPTER 1

# THE BARRIERS BETWEEN

I think that all of us could start with the premise that there are three participants present in every witnessing endeavor. I'm sure that we will all agree with this in theory if not in practice! As a matter of fact, my contention has always been that though we all profess to believe this in theory, it has in reality not made it into our practice. Those three participants are of course the witness, The Holy Spirit, and the sinner. A successful witnessing encounter will attach a vehicle to each of these three participants. The vehicle of the witness is Truth, the vehicle of The Holy Spirit is Conviction, and the vehicle of the sinner is Repentance.

The vehicle of truth that is used by the witness is, of course, the Bible! We see this vehicle in John 17:17, **"Sanctify them through thy truth: thy word is truth,"** and also in 2 Timothy 2:15, **"Study to shew thyself approved unto God, a workman that needeth not to be ashamed, rightly dividing the word of truth."** This vehicle can further be substantiated through the parable of the sower in

Mark 4:14, **"The sower soweth the word."** When you and I approach a sinner with the subject of his or her never-dying soul, may we never substitute the truth of God with the traditions of men!

When we look at the second participant, The Holy Spirit, we of course acknowledge that the vehicle through which He works is that of conviction. His job description is outlined in John 16:8, **"And when he is come, he will reprove the world of sin, and of righteousness, and of judgment:"** The outworking of that process is described by Jesus Himself in John 6:44, **"No man can come to me, except the Father which hath sent me draw him: and I will raise him up at the last day."** This description of conviction is now and has always been assigned to The Holy Ghost.

The last party of our trio also has a responsibility. The vehicle attached to the sinner is that of repentance. Our Lord Himself addresses the issue in Luke 13 with two identical verses (3 and 5) that say, **"I tell you, Nay: but, except ye repent, ye shall all likewise perish."** It was obvious to the first century church that repentance was a necessary vehicle in the response of a sinner as evidenced in the Book of Acts. **"Testifying both to the Jews, and also to the Greeks, repentance toward God, and faith toward our Lord Jesus Christ."** Acts 20:21 **"But shewed first unto them of Damascus, and at Jerusalem, and**

**throughout all the coasts of Judea, and *then* to the Gentiles, that they should repent and turn to God, and do works meet for repentance."** Acts 26:20 **"And the times of this ignorance God winked at; but commandeth all men every where to repent:"** Acts 17:30.

The evidence in the Bible for the need of repentance is so overwhelming, that I almost cringe to think that there are those who disagree with its necessity! Perhaps the divisiveness of this issue rests in a disagreement of definition. The best description that I have ever heard is that repentance is a change of heart that results in a change of direction. I have no trouble with this definition in light of the fact that many times when salvation is spoken of in the scriptures, there is also a reference to the heart. Couple that with the fact that 2 Corinthians 5:15 states, **"Therefore if any man *be* in Christ, *he is* a new creature: old things are passed away; behold, all things are become new."** Sounds to me like a change of heart that results in a change of direction!

Now let me show you the barriers that have come between the participants and the vehicles. As you might expect, these barriers have not been moved into place by God! Since He is **"...not willing than any should perish, but that all should come to repentance."** (2 Peter 3:9), you can rest assured that that it is not His heavenly construction equipment that moves barriers into place! These man-made barriers are illustrated below.

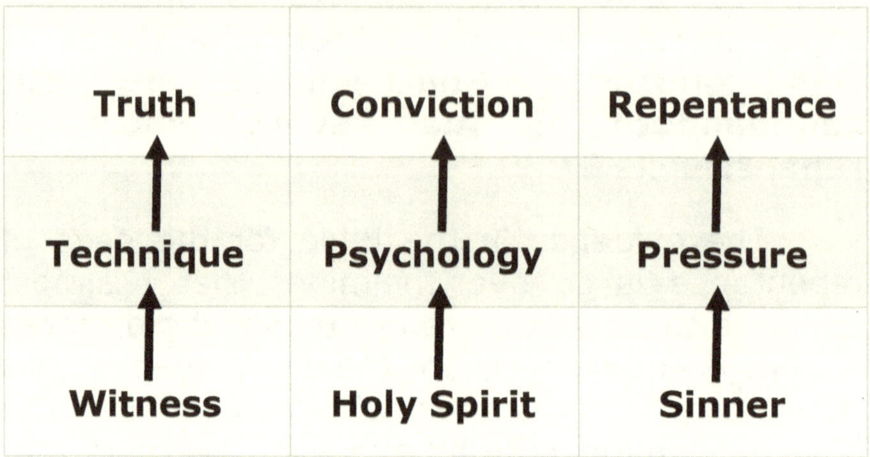


You will note that unlike the last illustration, we now have something that has come between the participant and the vehicle. These barriers have been placed there in order to keep the participant from yoking up with the vehicle! When this man-made substitute process is placed into motion, you are now more likely to produce a false profession than a genuine salvation experience! And before you take issue with me over that statement, take a little survey in some of our Independent Baptist Churches, and compare the number of "professions of faith" with the number of converts in the pews! You'll find it is to be somewhat like that missionary who had 738 professions of faith and 25 baptisms this past year.

Although various practices of these barriers will appear in future chapters of this book, I will address them partially as I close this chapter, so that you will be on the lookout for them throughout the book. Technique is very simply those teachings that have made their way into our soul-winning arena that have absolutely no basis in scripture. As a matter-of-fact, some of them are even contrary to biblical principle! Very simply put, soul-winning is not a technique, but rather the acting out of scriptural principle on the subject of sharing your faith.

Psychology on the other hand has become man's substitute for the convicting power of The Holy Spirit. Its design is to manipulate the mind by way of the participant known as the witness, instead of allowing the participant, The Holy Spirit, to work with the vehicle of conviction. Not only does it bypass the Holy Spirit, its use also bypasses the recipient's heart, thus imparting an intellectual knowledge, which alone will not produce repentance! Let's keep in mind that it is conviction that produces repentance, and conviction is assigned to The Holy Spirit alone!

The barrier of pressure has been placed between the sinner and repentance. And once again, it is used by the participant known as the witness. For a firsthand experience of this folly, you need only to examine the average Baptist evangelist's invitation! That is not to exclude the overzealous soul-winner nor the technique-plagued pastor. Let me note at this time that this author is not opposed to the use of a "challenge" in a soul-winning encounter, such as the use of James 4:14, **"Whereas ye know not what *shall***

***be* on the morrow. For what *is* your life? It is even a vapour, that appeareth for a little time, and then vanisheth away."** To warn someone of the brevity of life is not pressure, but rather heartfelt concern toward someone who has indicated that they will think about the matter of their soul later. There is a fine line between pressure and challenge, and one must be led by the Holy Spirit as to when that line has been crossed. Of course, when the Holy Spirit has been replaced by the barrier of psychology, there is not much chance of knowing when you have crossed that line!

Every "Soul-Winning Course" that I have ever been exposed to, has been riddled with these three barriers, leaving the blessed Holy Spirit out in the cold and the sinner sitting on his hands! The soul-winner, which I prefer to refer to as the witness, is basically taught to do the job of all three participants, thus producing the multitudes of false professions that we seem to enjoy boasting about. And, even more discouraging than the three barriers of technique, psychology, and pressure, I have witnessed the intermingling of trickery and dishonesty on many occasions! I will also address these issues before we close the last chapter of the book.

# CHAPTER 2
# UNREASONABLE GOALS

Throughout the years of my salvation, I have heard on many occasions, pastors and evangelists encouraging laymen to set goals, for the upcoming year, for the number of people they wish to "lead to Christ." Sometimes it is a goal to "win" so many each week during their soul-winning time. And, of course, there are those laymen who set those goals for themselves without the encouragement or challenge of some preacher. This certainly sounds commendable and worthy of our consideration, were it not for the fact that it is terribly unscriptural! Although I am sure that the motive may be honorable, its propagation comes about as a result of the misuse of terminology and/or scriptural doctrine. This is why I made the statement earlier that I prefer to use the title of "witness" rather than "soul-winner."

Preachers teaching the Bible "out of context" in such cases as Proverbs 11:30, have led people to believe that it is the witness that imparts everlasting life, and not the Holy Ghost. The verse reads, **"The fruit of the righteous *is* a tree of life; and he that winneth souls *is* wise."** That can be very confusing on the surface, which is why God encourages us to never study Bible doctrine on the surface, but rather compare scripture with scripture and never base a doctrine on an isolated verse or passage! When heeding the admonition of 2 Timothy 2:15, **"Study to shew thyself approved unto God, a workman that needeth not to be ashamed, rightly dividing the word of truth"**, one would not make the mistake of thinking that they "win the soul."

Rightly dividing the word of truth on the doctrine of whose responsibility it is to "win" a sinner to Christ, or who imparts the passage of eternal life to a lost soul, would bring you to only one conclusion. That conclusion is best stated in 1 Corinthians 3:6 and 7, **"I have planted, Apollos watered; but God gave the increase. So then neither is he that planteth any thing, neither he that watereth; but God that giveth the increase."** Or even Jesus' teaching in John 6:44, **"No man can come to me, except the Father which hath sent me draw him: and I will raise him up at the last day."** I hope, dear reader, that you don't think you are the one who does the "drawing" that Jesus is speaking of in that verse!

So then, if brother so-n-so taught me that I am the one who wins souls (which is probably where we get the terminology soul-winner), but God says that it is the Holy Spirit, and I am simply the messenger boy, who is right? Doing a thorough study on the subject would bring you and I to a sane, coherent conclusion. The wise man is he who has decided to partner with the Holy Spirit, allow himself to be the bearer of truth, giving opportunity for the Holy Spirit to work through him and through His Word, producing conviction (which is the responsibility of the Holy Spirit), which could in turn produce repentance (which is the responsibility of the sinner). And, yes, if you will avail yourself to be a part of that divine plan, God would certainly consider you to be wise! But while you are "planting" and "watering," don't be so foolish as to take credit for "the increase!"

With these thoughts in mind, let's turn our attention once again to "unreasonable goals." If I were a sports commentator interviewing a football team before a big game, and my lot was to question the players concerning their anticipated performance during the game, what would I expect to hear from each position? What if, in the process of speaking with the field goal kicker, I asked him what his goals are for the game, and he responds, "My goal is to gain over 200 yards passing." My first comment would probably be, "How is that possible when you are not the quarterback but rather the field goal kicker?" I think that we could all agree that this man's goals are unreasonable! His goals must remain within the confines of his position, and not the position of someone else on his team! As a matter-of-fact, there would be a strong possibility that the quarterback would be a little "put out" by his teammate's goal!

Do we not understand how the Holy Spirit must be thinking when we set our goals not on our position, but on His? If He is the one who gives "the increase" – the participant who is responsible for the conviction, I believe I'll let Him take care of His own goals! I know some evangelists who would do well to keep this principle in mind during the invitation time! Does that mean that I should have no goals as a participant in the soul-winning process? Not at all – but your goals should be in line with the vehicle that God has given you as a participant of the process. To refresh your memory, you are the witness and your vehicle is truth. You must live the truth, walk the truth, study the truth, memorize the truth, and give out the truth. Let's talk about some responsible goals on your behalf.

Since you "planteth: and "watereth," your goals should fit within that realm. A reasonable goal on your part could be to pass out so many tracts this year, or per week, or to never go a day without handing out a gospel tract; or, in similar fashion, to knock on so many doors this year, this week, or perhaps this month. Maybe it would be to never miss church visitation on the designated evening. Another worthy goal could be to try to engage someone in spiritual conversation every day of your life. Keep in mind that the best way to strengthen the truth as you share it, is to be sure that you are walking in truth before those who you are sharing it with! This is especially true in your own community and among your own family, co-workers, or friends.

Maybe you would choose to set a goal to witness to everyone in your high school graduating class. Or, perhaps, to be a witness to everyone in your workplace. How about giving a tract to every retailer whose store you frequent? All of the above mentioned are obtainable goals and are in the sphere of your responsibility, but don't cross the line and insist on doing the convicting for the Holy Spirit, or the repenting for the sinner! When you get out of your vehicle, and start driving the other two, you are destined for a spiritual wreck! You are more apt to produce a false profession, give someone a false assurance of their salvation, and push a soul into hell!

Many years ago, in order to answer the criticism of mounting up so many false professions, I heard a brother say, "I would rather lead 100 souls to Christ, knowing that 95 of them were false professions, and see 5 of them go to heaven, than to not attempt to be a soul-winner." The first tragedy of that statement is assuming that those are the only two options! Either to rack up false professions while winning a few, or to not witness at all! (How about the option of being a witness within the guidelines of scriptural teachings - which produces very few false professions!) The second tragedy is the flippant attitude about the 95 people who you gave the assurance of their salvation that will one day wake up in hell! Most of them will not let a genuine witness to approach them about their soul, because they're banking on that false assurance that you gave them!

If your attitude is similar to that of this brother's, let someone else reach those 5, and probably the majority of the other 95, with the use of proper scriptural principles. The thought that fits best on that subject is found in 2 Peter 2: 20 and 21, **"For if after they have escaped the pollutions of the world through the knowledge of the Lord and Saviour Jesus Christ, they are again entangled therein, and overcome, the latter end is worse with them than the beginning. For it had been better for them not to have known the way of righteousness, then, after they have known *it*, to turn from the holy commandment delivered unto them."** Of course my whole point of this chapter is to help you see that when you are trying to accomplish goals that belong to the Holy Spirit and not you, your likelihood of causing a fiasco is pretty good!

# CHAPTER 3
# REWARDING RESULTS?

That brings us to the erroneous teaching, that, in the matter of soul-winning, God rewards results. This often comes by way of the illustration of the soul-winner's crown. How many times have I heard it suggested by some preacher that when you lead a soul to Christ, God puts another jewel in your crown? Do I think that there will be a reward in heaven for those who attempt to witness their faith to the lost? – Yes! Do I think that those rewards will be based upon how many folks get saved as a result of their witness? – No! Since the convicting is not my job, and the repentance is not my job, why would God condition my reward upon those results? To carefully consider this issue, let's go to two witnesses found in the Bible.

The two that I refer to are Noah and Jonah. Both of these men heralded the message of a righteous God and the coming judgment upon sinners. Jonah's preaching resulted in the salvation of what theologians estimate to be hundreds of thousands of souls. Noah, on the other hand preached for 120 years, with the sum total of 0 walking the isle! With the exception of his own family, Noah never had a convert! Which of these two had the distinctive honor of being elevated into God's "Hall of Faith" found in Hebrews chapter eleven? Yes, Noah, the one with the least results!

If rewards are based upon results, that would mean that the preacher that God placed in a heavily populated metropolitan area, has a distinct advantage toward earning rewards for his labors, over the preacher that God placed in a sparsely populated farming region. Why would God give one a greater advantage that the other, when it comes to earning eternal rewards? It seems as though that would be a pretty uneven playing field for a God who is said to have **"...no respect of persons..."** (Romans 2:11).

Whether-or-not someone gets saved, is based upon all three participants fulfilling their task. The Holy Spirit will definitely do His part (if I don't try to take His place), I must do my part in bearing the message, and the sinner must do his part by putting his faith and trust in Christ. You mean to tell me that if the sinner refuses to get saved, I get no reward for carrying out my part? Since when does God attach one man's reward to another man's obedience? Let's settle on the fact that God rewards faithfulness and obedience, and not results! What saith the scriptures **"...to obey *is* better than sacrifice,..."** (1 Samuel 15:22) and, in Matthew 25:21, **"...Well done, *thou* good and faithful servant:..."**

Placing rewards in proper perspective would change the scene in most churches and Baptist Bible Colleges. Instead of praising the person who succeeded in getting the most people to "pray after him," we would be praising the person, or persons, who delivered the gospel message the most times! We envision "success" in respect to the number of people who responded positively to our witness, while God describes success as being faithful and obedient to delivering the message, regardless of the sinner's decision. Point and case – Noah and Jonah! When Bible colleges elect "Miss and Mr. So-n-So," from their student body, their main criteria is based on how many people they "led to Christ." Poor Noah wouldn't have had a chance! Does it ever occur to them that they are rewarding the wrong participant and the wrong vehicle?

Why is it so important to get this reward issue put in its proper perspective? Because once you convince someone that they are going to be rewarded for their own results, they are now more apt to cross the line of trying to do the job of the Holy Spirit or of the lost sinner, thus producing a false profession, and a false hope for heaven! In the two churches that I formerly pastored, I always emphasized that a successful witness is not one accepted – but one given. The degree of your success does not increase one iota because the recipient gets saved. Your success is only measured by your part of the encounter, and your part is to deliver the message!

# CHAPTER 4

# THE ILLUSIVE SINNER'S PRAYER

I hate to butcher this "sacred cow," but the fact remains that it is one of the most misused man-made doctrines in our Baptist toolbox! As far as I can gather, its origin comes from the parable of the Pharisee and the publican, in Luke, chapter 18. The teaching, is the contrast between self-righteousness, and true humility. The conclusion is that humility produces justification and a salvation experience. To dub that "the sinner's prayer" by declaring one who repeats that prayer to be "saved," is to do a great injustice to Bible teaching. There are countless numbers of prayers and statements made by people in the Bible, just before, or attached to, their salvation experience, none of which has the power to save an individual!

Why don't we take the statement made by the woman at the well, in John 4:29, **"Come, see a man, which told me all things that ever I did: is not this the Christ?"** Or, the thief on the cross, in Luke 23:42, **"And he said unto Jesus, Lord, remember me when thou comest into thy kingdom."** Would it not be appropriate to use Zacchaeus' statement, in Luke 19:8, **"And Zacchaeus stood, and said unto the Lord; Behold Lord, the half of my goods I give to the poor; and if I have taken anything from any man by false accusation, I restore *him* fourfold."** All of these statements, and many more, were significant in revealing a changed heart that resulted in a salvation experience, but, none are a magic wand for others to use them to gain an access to heaven!

The church that I now attend recently had an evangelist make a statement during his message that he later violated by the time he got to his "invitation." He was speaking of the fabricated practices of Roman Catholics, which have no evidence in scriptures. Purgatory happened to be the subject of his scorn, as he shared with us that he has had the dubious pleasure of offering any Catholic $1,000.00, if they can give him the scriptures that justify such an existence. He proceeded to tell us that he has made that a standing offer for the last 20 years and has never had a "taker." His whole point was the terrible atrocity of adding man-made teachings and religious practices that have no foundation in scripture. As a converted Roman Catholic, I have no problem with his statements or train of thought. But, as a Biblicist, I do have a problem with the hypocrisy that followed!

During his invitation, with "heads bowed and eyes closed," he led people in a "sinner's prayer," assuring them that if they prayed (that prayer) after him, they were now children of God and had the assurance of a place in heaven because **"Whosoever shall call upon the name of the Lord shall be saved."** Of course he didn't bother telling them that he was now practicing something that he earlier railed on the Catholics for doing!

He was now in the midst of placing something into religious practice that has no scriptural basis! I'll give him the same $1,000.00 if he can show me someone in the Bible who ever "led' someone else in a "sinner's prayer!" While he was removing the "mote" from the Catholic's eyes, he neglected to see the "beam" that was in his own! If it's wrong for a Catholic to fabricate rituals and practices – it's wrong for a Baptist! His need may be to take a closer look at Romans 2:21, **"Thou therefore which teachest another, teachest thou not thyself? Thou that preachest a man should not steal, doest thou steal?"**

Is this practice really that bad? It is when you're "messing with someone's forever" as stated by that layman in Wisconsin. A sinner under conviction by The Holy Ghost, who desires to repent and make things right with God, will cry out without any need of your instruction! The reason that we find it necessary to intercede with such a prayer, is because there is no conviction nor repentance on the scene. I suggest that you and I wait until the other two participants use their vehicles, and the sinner crying out to God will take care of itself! Besides, do you have any idea of the sweet prayers that you are cheating yourself out of hearing, when you interfere with man's practices? You may go on "leading" people in "the sinner's prayer," but you have no Bible justification for it! Keep in mind that the very model prayer taken from Luke 18 that is used in this man-made process; that the publican who said it was not "led" in that prayer! It was said from his own heart to God's ear. Your attempt to get a feather in your hat, could push a soul into hell!

## CHAPTER 5

## FARMING OR RETAIL SALES?

One could certainly approach the act of witnessing or soul-winning in the wrong fashion, if they are misled as to what it is likened in the Bible. As a matter of fact, many of the lectures that I have heard through the years would definitely sway a person to the wrong approach. I remember hearing "one of America's leading soul-winners" comment during teaching that the most time that it should ever take a person to win a soul to Christ would never exceed twenty minutes. No wonder people push for decisions on their first encounter with a lost person! That would also cause a witness to stray from his own responsibility into the area of the Holy Spirit's and the sinner's.

My guess is that the Apostle Paul didn't catch this fellow's lecture, as evidenced with his work with Felix in Acts 24:26, **"...wherefore he sent for him the oftener, and communed with him."** The Bible examples that exceeded twenty minutes would cause us to bore you to death, if we took the time to draw them all to your attention. Witnessing is not what many would have you to believe, a few minutes start to finish, and you will lead people to a genuine conversion on a regular basis. That sounds more like retail sales than the illustration of farming that the Bible so often refers to. That is also why people try to do the responsibility of all three participants instead of staying in the realm of their own! Retail sales also lends itself to pressure and psychology, as most of you readers are aware of. On the other hand, farming requires neither!

How soon we forget the parable of The Sower and The Seed. Or Paul's description in 1 Corinthians 3:5-7, **"Who then is Paul, and who *is* Apollos, but ministers by whom ye believed, even as the Lord gave to every man? I have planted, Apollos watered; but God gave the increase. So then neither is he that planteth any thing, neither he that watereth; but God that giveth the increase."** I suggest that you ask any farmer if you can plant, water, and harvest in twenty minutes! And, as with different crops, people differ in the amount of time it takes to plant, water, or harvest. Similar also to farming, there are times that you may have to replant a crop! When I approach a soul, I never know if the seed has been planted, nor how much it has been watered if it is planted, but I definitely know that both are required before there can be a harvest! A spirit-filled witness will discern whether or not the sinner's "ground" has been worked on before. The best way to foil a situation is to plant when you should be watering, or water when there needs to be planting, or to try to force a harvest when they are not ready, refusing to realize that that's not your task anyway!

To compound the problem, we have all these "super soul-winners" writing books that give an account of their soul-winning experiences that reads like an instruction manual on retail sales. There are two things that they do not tell you. One is, what might have transpired in the recipient's life before they even came on the scene, and the other was whether or not these individuals ever darkened the door of a church! Let me write about one of my personal experiences much the way they would, and show you the confusion that could result.

Several years ago, another fellow and I embarked on an evening of visitation in a small country town in Iowa where I pastored my first church. After much prayer and driving, I arrived at a neighborhood where I began to feel peace and so parked the car. Our destination seemed to be this small trailer court where I found myself knocking on the first door. When no one answered the door, we moved to the second trailer where I was greeted by a middle-aged woman. After my very brief introduction, she threw the door open and stated that she had been waiting for me. As always I tried to begin the conversation with some small talk, but was abrupty interrupted by her comment, "I need for you to tell me how to get saved!" In a very brief period of time, I led the dear lady to faith in Christ, and yes, she became a very faithful member of my church.

If I leave the story there, it gives the retail sales impression, and others will go after the same experience. But, as Paul Harvey says, "And now for the rest of the story." After her encounter with Christ, she shared with me that she had just returned from Georgia, where she had been called upon to help an ailing sister for nearly three months. During this three month period, her saved sister witnessed to her on several occasions. She persuaded her to attend her Baptist church on a regular basis while she was there. Her pastor visited and witnessed to her on more than one occasion. She assured her sister that though she wouldn't get saved then, that she would look into a church that taught the same thing when she got back home to Iowa, and perhaps get saved then. She barely got her luggage unpacked before I came to the door!

The planting was done, the watering was done, the conviction was present and the repentance was well on its way. All I had to do was to show up and witness the harvest! With the "rest of the story" it is obvious that what appeared on the surface to be a retail sale, was indeed a farming process. Don't misunderstand what I am saying – I am not saying that salvation is a process. Salvation occurs instantaneous the moment someone repents and turns to the Saviour and what He did in their place at Calvary! However, to get the recipient to that moment takes a process that the Bible refers to as planting and watering! To treat the matter otherwise is to suggest that a person is mindless and heartless.

I have had those who have implied that the conversion experience of the Apostle Paul refutes what I am saying in this chapter. After all, his salvation story on the road to Damascus was instantaneous and contained no planting and watering. How soon some have forgotten his presence two chapters earlier in Acts at the stoning of Stephen! Deep was the seed planted by a young martyr who spent his last breath asking God to forgive their actions. Within ear shot of that prayer was Saul of Tarsus, later to be known as the Apostle Paul. You and I will never know this side of heaven how much watering was added to that seed by other Christians whom Saul sent to prison for their faith.

The reason my church growth far outweighed those who prayed with me during a soul-winning encounter, was because I didn't consider soul-winning as a retail sales process, but rather a farming experience. Sitting on the front of my office desk were two file boxes containing the names of folks who I was working with. I referred to them as my "farming boxes" and treated them as such. In a later book I am writing entitled, "Fruit in your Basket" I will go into greater detail as to how I worked those boxes in my farming experiences.

# CHAPTER 6
# SNEAK UP ON THEM

Lying somewhere between psychology and insanity enters the teaching that you should never carry a Bible where it is visible and can be seen by your "victim." Of course, the thought is that you are more apt to get in someone's house if they don't know what you are there for! Has it ever occurred to you that if they have no interest in the things of God, it won't change because of your deception. As a matter of fact, you could save yourself a lot of time by letting people know up front why you are there! If they have no interest and refuse to let you in; that will allow you better spent time walking down the street to find someone who does. The idea that we can trick people into having an interest in spiritual things, who would otherwise not have, by simply "hiding our sword" defies the very concept that an individual must surrender their will to God before they can be saved!

When admonished by God to **"Put on the whole armour of God..."** (Ephesians 6:11) do you really think that any part of that armour is to be hidden? As (He includes) **"...the sword of the Spirit, which is the word of God:"**, is there any indication in that text that we are to hide that particular object that we might "sneak up" on the enemy? I have found two very good reasons for me to carry my sword where people can see it. One is, I have always felt better about an honest approach in being straightforward with people, and they too have felt better about me being honest about my approach. And the second is, occasion has found me in neighborhoods that my main source of safety has been the visibility of my Bible! It has probably become evident to you that I favor Elijah's approach with the 450 false prophets of Baal as he "laid his cards on the table" and did business for God.

Throughout my life as a Christian, I have seen this deceptive "sneak-up-on-them" approach cause irreversible damage to those that it has been used on. A pastor friend of mine in Minnesota secured a meeting with a marshal-art expert for a service in a large public auditorium. When the guest speaker had the posters made, he neglected to mention that the services would include a gospel presentation. Although my pastor friend was not comfortable with this approach, he was assured that this method has always increased the crowd and the results. When the meeting "changed gears" the verbal abuse and gestures from the audience foiled and chances of any kind of a successful spiritual outcome! As a matter of fact you could say that they came much closer to a riot than to a revival! Even though lost people are being deceived by Satan, they don't appreciate being deceived by God's people! A full year after the incident, that local pastor will still trying to gain back the confidence of the community. You see, not everyone appreciates being "snuck up on!"

# CHAPTER 7

# STAY ON THE SUBJECT?

I wish I had a dime for every time that I heard this taught in a soul-winning lecture. Although I think that the intent is probably good, once again the Scriptures don't always bare our man-made teaching! Of course we should always remember why we are there in the first place, and keep our goal of presenting the gospel in the forefront of our minds. I also agree that our efforts should never be just "visitation" but an opportunity to share the saving grace of Jesus Christ. However, there are some people who are going to insist on getting answers to their earnest questions before you can proceed with your mission. You have probably been instructed to say something like "That's a good question Joe, and I'll be happy to answer that for you as soon as you allow me to finish the subject that we are on." The instruction is to never let the recipient move you off the subject. That's good if you are planning on a one-sided conversation and the other individual is not allowed to participate!

I've even heard a lecturer go so far as to say, "After you've led them to Christ they probably won't remember that question anyway, so don't bring it up again." Then why did you tell them that you would answer it after you were through? Another form of deception? There are often times when obstacles stand in the way of people getting saved, and you would do well to deal with those obstacles in order to move them closer to the cross. It might interest you to know that there are scriptural teachings to that end.

Have you ever studied Paul's approach with Felix in Acts 24:24 and 25? There you will read, **"And after certain days, when Felix came with his wife Drusilla, which was a Jewess, he sent for Paul, and heard him concerning the faith in Christ. And as he reasoned of righteousness, temperance, and judgment to come, Felix trembled, and answered, Go thy way for this time; when I have a convenient season, I will call for thee."** How many Bible subjects could you fit into "righteousness" and "temperance?" Enough to understand that Paul didn't "stay on the subject!" We have no indication that Felix ever got saved, but we do know that the Apostle Paul spoke to him about a variety of subjects. I have more confidence in Paul's soul-winning course than I do in most of the brethren's today!

I want you to note Jesus' teachings concerning thinking things over before spiritual decisions are made, **"For which of you, intending to build a tower, sitteth not down first, and counteth the cost, whether he have sufficient to finish it? Lest haply, after he hath laid the foundation, and is not able to finish it, all that behold it begin to mock him, Saying, This man began to build, and was not able to finish, Or what king, going to make war against another king, sitteth not down**

**first, and consulteth whether he be able with ten thousand to meet him that cometh against him with twenty thousand? Or else, while the other is yet a great way off, he sendeth an ambassage, and desireth conditions of peace. So likewise, whosoever he be of you that forsaketh not all that he hath, he cannot be my disciple."** Luke 14:28-33. Are we foolish enough to think that Jesus encourages people to "count the cost" of being His disciple, but would not encourage a lost man to "count the cost" of becoming a Christian? When they ask sincere questions it is usually part of the process of them "counting the cost." Sometimes in order to obey some soul-winner's lecture about "staying on the subject," we are failing to "meet the need" of a recipient who is simply "counting the cost" of his or her spiritual decision!

# CHAPTER 8

# THE NUMBERS RACKET

It seems as though you can't have a Baptist pastors' fellowship without hearing all kinds of numbers being thrown around! I've heard all the justification for it, such as, "The Bible is full of numbers," or, "We know how many got saved at Pentecost," and many such like statements, "So it must be all right to record our number of salvations." What they neglect to recognize about Pentecost is that Peter is not the one making the announcement! As a matter of fact, I challenge you to find someone in the Bible who makes any kind of a statement as to the number of people they "led to the Lord." I don't want to sound too Biblical in our observations, but isn't the Bible supposed to be our guide? Since this practice isn't generated scripturally, shouldn't we arrive at the conclusion that it must be man-made?

I have heard it said, "It is unfortunate that Brother So-n-So didn't keep adequate records of those that he led to faith in Christ, so we can only estimate." Has it ever occurred to you that that brother may have noticed that there was no such thing in the Bible and therefore didn't go down that road? And at the risk of sounding like a broken record, why would I keep track of what isn't even my responsibility? If I were keeping records, it should be of the planting and watering – not the increase! I choose to let the Holy Spirit keep His own records! Don't you? When I first went into the field of evangelism, a Baptist periodical dropped my ad because I refused to given them the number of "results" from my meetings. I'm so glad that I chose this path early on, so that I was never tempted to lie about my meetings like the evangelist I spoke of in the forward of this book!

If I understand the Great Commission correctly (Matthew 28:18-20), our responsibility is to get people saved, then baptized, and then get them into church where they can learn the Word. (It seems to me like there are a lot of "bragging tallies" going around out there about only one-third of the Great Commission!) You'll note that the Holy Spirit didn't turn loose of that number at Pentecost until all three parts of The Great Commission were fulfilled in those lives! Yes, 3,000 got saved, 3,000 got baptized, and 3,000 got into church! A little different than the missionary letter we talked about earlier where 738 got saved, 25 got baptized, and embarrassment probably caused him to omit the number of those 25 that were still in church!

Do as I have done and ponder David's great sin in numbering the people. What made the sin so enormous that 70,000 people died as a result? We can all agree on the fact that it resulted from an act of disobedience, but why did God forbid it to be done, and what drove David to do it? The context and circumstances seem to bring us to a logical conclusion. Measuring his great conquering successes, David wanted the number of soldiers with which he had accomplished such tactical defeats. What he failed to remember is that it was not manpower, nor his strategies on the battlefield, but rather The God Who led and instructed him! We are talking about a God Who will give His Glory to no one, nor allow anyone else to take it! I submit to you that those who have embarked on the numbers racket are committing the same sin as David! If it is God **"who giveth the increase,"** then why are we attaching those numbers to ourselves, thus taking the glory from God? **"And David's heart smote him after that he had numbered the people. And David said unto the LORD, I have sinned greatly in that I have done: and now, I beseeh thee, O LORD, take away the iniquity of thy servant; for I have done very foolishly."** (2 Samuel 24:10) Try that "sinner's prayer!"

# CHAPTER 9
# THE PRESENCE OF REPENTANCE

There are so many books now available on the subject that I hesitate treading upon this ground. I do, however, want to cover the issue well enough to help you to understand that where there is no repentance, there is no salvation! The controversy may come over the definition of repentance and not its need. At least I hope that because the evidence is so overwhelming in the Scriptures, that none of our dear readers are stubborn enough to think that it is not a necessary part of the new birth! Even though all of us won't come up with the same word-for-word definition of the act of repentance, we should all agree that once enacted, it causes a life changing result! When the largest percentage of our "converts" have no desire to follow the Lord in believers' baptism, or even to come to church the first time, perhaps it's time we come to the conclusion that there was no repentance!

Two classic examples of repentance occur in the Bible, one in the Old Testament and one in the New. Each make it evident the repentance is both visible and life changing. One takes place in the shadow of the cross, as Jesus hangs between the two thieves. The two thieves are mentioned in all four of the gospels and produce a narrative that some nonbelievers insist is a contradiction. Matthew and Mark record how the two reviled and mocked Him as did the priests and Pharisees.

John mentions no narrative; only that they were there. Luke chapter 23, however, tells of the repentant thief what called upon The Saviour, asking Him to **"...remember me when thou comest into thy kingdom."** This is not a contradiction as some suppose it to be, but rather an illustration of repentance played out in the life of that thief. Is this not a "change of heart resulting in a change of direction" as some define repentance to be? And is it not evident to all who witness it? Can you not see the indisputable picture? It is the Gospel that saves, and as that Gospel is actually being carried out - God places repentance right in the middle of it!

Then there is the story of Jonah and Nineveh in the Old Testament. A city and people so wicked that God sent a preacher to tell them that He was about to wipe them off the face of the earth. The preacher, Jonah, didn't even care if they got saved. The fact is, he was very disappointed when they did! This shows you and I that it is not the attitude of the soul-winner, but the actions of the recipient that produces repentance. After the message was given, the admonition was then given by the king himself, **"But let man and beast be covered with sackcloth, and cry mightily unto God: yea, let them turn every one from his evil way, and from the violence that is in their hands."** (Jonah 3:8) Doing so, we see the results in verse 10, **"And God saw their works, that they turned from their evil way; and God repented of the evil, that he**

**had said that he would do unto them; and he did it not." "They turned from their evil way,"** which makes a pretty good definition of repentance! If it is true that repentance means a changed heart and a changed mind resulting in a new direction – the Ninevites had exactly that!

Mind you, these are not the only two examples in the Bible, but they are surely classic ones. This is especially true at the cross. We see repentance being acted out right in the middle of the Gospel! The admonition of repentance is given much in the New Testament, without being attached to a story. To save time and space in this book, and to satisfy your own heart concerning this vital subject, I suggest that you do a word study on the subject. My favorite, will probably always be Jesus' words in Luke 13:3 and 5, **"I tell you, Nay: but, except ye repent, ye shall all likewise perish."** Both verses read exactly the same, and as I heard a man once say, "God never repeats Himself because He ran out of things to say, but rather because He wants to add emphasis to what He has said!"

One of the reasons I am opposed to the witness monopolizing the conversation, is because, I believe that repentance comes about, or can be discerned through the recipient's involvement. If you treat someone like they are mindless and speechless beings, and control their answers and conversation – as most "soul-winning" manuals instruct you to do, you are very apt to produce a false profession. It's kind of like being manipulated by a high pressure salesman, and later regretting that you ever bought the product! You have a "silent salesman" (The Holy Ghost) who will never pressure a person beyond their free will, and if you and I will allow Him to do His work, He will produce the conviction that will result in repentance.

# CHAPTER 10

# ARE WE PREACHING REPENTANCE?

I recently asked a Baptist pastor if he ever explained to a lost sinner, the doctrine of repentance. It was no shock to me that he responded that he never went into detail on that subject when trying to win someone to Christ. Of course, just like so many others, he felt that his responsibility is to preach the Gospel. That sounds good on the surface, until you begin to meditate on some scriptural principles!

Let's examine some passages of Scripture to see if preaching the Gospel releases us from all other commands. Begin with Luke 24:47 **"And that repentance and remission of sins should be preached in his name among all nations, beginning at Jerusalem."** We all know that to preach simply means to declare a truth. If we are to preach or declare the Gospel to a lost sinner, could someone tell me why we are not supposed to do likewise concerning repentance? If God did not want repentance preached or declared then why did He command us to do so?

Listen to Paul's declaration to the church members at Ephesus in Acts 20:20 and 21, **"And how I kept back nothing that was profitable unto you, but have shewed you, and have taught you publickly, and from house to house, Testifying both to the Jews, and also to the Greeks, repentance toward God, and faith toward our Lord Jesus Christ."** While the

Apostle Paul said that repentance was "profitable," the average "soul-winner" today doesn't think that it is important enough to even bring the subject up when working with a lost soul! He "testified" repentance to the lost, while today's preacher doesn't think that it's necessary to even mention it.

In light of Jesus' declaration that we mentioned earlier in Luke chapter 13, verses 3 and 5, **"I tell you, Nay: but, except ye repent, ye shall all likewise perish,"** why is it that we don't even talk to the sinner about it? We are supposedly trying to keep the individual from "perishing," but we are not encouraged to tell them what that word "repent" means. If this is the act that Jesus said would keep them from perishing, then I suggest, you and I take the time to explain to them what repentance is! That means preach repentance to them as you have been commanded!

Have you ever asked yourself why God thought that it was necessary to preach repentance to the sinner? Could it be that the reason may be found in Jesus' teachings at Luke 14:28-33, **"For which of you, intending to build a tower, sitteth not down first, and counteth the cost, whether he have sufficient to finish it? Lest haply, after he hath laid the foundation, and is not able to finish it, all that behold it begin to mock him, Saying, This man began to build, and was not able to finish. Or what king, going to make**

**war against another king, sitteth not down first, and consulteth whether he be able with ten thousand to meet him that cometh against him with twenty thousand? Or else, while the other is yet a great way off, he sendeth an ambassage, and desireth conditions of peace. So likewise, whosoever he be of you that forsaketh not all that he hath, he cannot be my disciple."** The teaching is clear! When making spiritual decisions – count the cost! The spiritual decision in this passage happens to be whether-or-not you want to be His disciple. Although some would argue that the passage is not talking about salvation but discipleship, my argument is why would He be any more concerned about you and I "counting the cost" of discipleship, than He would be about the spiritual decision of salvation?

Explaining what repentance means helps the sinner to "count the cost" of his or her decision about salvation! They need to understand that it means a change of heart that will result in a change of direction! Since when is it wrong to share 2 Corinthians 5:17 with a lost man? **"Therefore in any man be in Christ, he is a new creature: old things are passed away; behold, all things are become new."** That verse sounds like repentance in a nutshell! I generally make a statement that goes something like this, "If Jesus can't do a better job with your life than you can, what's the point in asking Him to come in?" Very simply put, I think that it is wrong to give a sinner the impression that they can take Jesus without taking His teachings! Dear friend, that's not works religion, nor Lordship salvation – that's repentance! You might find it necessary to explain to the sinner that they will still make mistakes, and that they will never arrive at perfection in this lifetime, but, in the same breath, you can also inform that same sinner that the Christian life is an honest effort to live by His teachings.

I contend that the sinner who believes that getting saved will not interfere with their present life, is not ready to repent, and you and I are better off to leave them alone until they are willing to count the cost! When repentance is included with the Gospel message, you are less likely to produce another false profession. Perhaps that is why we are commanded to preach both the Gospel and Repentance! When repentance becomes part of our message, you'll see less reports like 738 saved and 25 baptized!

## CHAPTER 11
## DISHONESTY AND PRESSURE

Nothing grieves the Holy Ghost of God more, than to look down upon a service, and see those "dirty tools" being used in what should be His work! By the way, if we trusted Him to do His work, we would never put our hands on these tools, as mechanics of spiritual truth! As the invitation is started, the pastor or evangelist asks everyone to "bow your head and close your eyes" usually followed by "no one is looking around for the privacy of this moment." Often I've heard them say "no one will single you out or embarrass you," or, something to that effect. The problem is – they are often lying! Someone on staff or certain laymen in the church are instructed to "peek" as the invitation is carried out. A typical instruction given to the sinner goes something like this, "If you were to die tonight, are you 100% sure that you will go to heaven? If not, would you slip up your hand, and, so doing, you are saying, 'Preacher pray for me, I'm not sure that if I died tonight I would go to heaven.'" Often, they assured once again that no one will come to them or embarrass them. Then, during the invitation time they are approached by someone – only to find out what liars we Christians are! Any time I have ever approached someone concerning this evil practice, I usually get a response that goes something like this, "You mean that you would let them die and go to hell?" You'll not put me on a guilt trip with your dishonesty! This business of "the end justifies the means" isn't within ten miles of old fashioned Holy Ghost conviction!

This wicked practice especially upsets this author, every time I think back and remember its application to someone very near and dear to me. For twenty years I prayed for my lost older brother, that he would come under the sound of the Gospel and give his life to Christ. He was a truck driver and spent much of his time on the road. Even though I shared with him, sometimes it takes another voice, when it comes to those nearest to you. In answer to my prayer, one day he parked his rig at a truck stop, looked through the local phone book to find a Baptist Church that might send someone out to pick him up for their services. As he told me this story, he remarked, "I thought that it was about time that I found out what this thing was that changed my little brother!" I was pretty excited about the story thus far, until he proceeded to tell me the rest. During the invitation time, the pastor went through the standard routine that I just explained, assuring everyone that "no one was looking around or would embarrass them." Well, to make a long story short, my brother did raise his hand for prayer," and as you might guess the assistant pastor tried to "pigeon hole" him during the invitation. Big brother sitting near the back of the church, threw our dishonest assistant pastor against the wall, assuring him that they were about to have to dig his teeth out of the sheetrock! In the process, he called him a few names, and used some choice language that I dare not print in this book! But don't get too excited about my brother's behavior, as you can expect lost people to act like that! God, however, doesn't expect saved people to act like that either, lying, you know. And, I'm sure that that pastor is in more trouble with God than my brother is over that particular incident!

Twenty years of prayer went right down the drain because of some manipulative, high pressure, dishonest Baptist pastor! I'm glad that my brother never told me the town, the church, nor the pastor's name! It would be very easy for me to get in the flesh and finish the job that my brother started. As of the writing of this book, that incident occurred 15 years ago – and my brother is still lost. Only now he has been given a good reason to stay away from Baptist churches! Someone out here has prayed for 20 years or more for their loved one's salvation. Please don't use deception to try to reach them. Let's leave deception to the devil and his crowd!

When I was in the pastorate, I hosted singing groups from Baptist Bible Colleges who were instructed in this trickery. Their chaperone or staff member would bring the message, giving the sinner the same assurance that "no one was looking around," while all along they were instructed to watch and then approach the lost person raising their hand during the invitation. That would happen just once in a church that I pastored, before I assured my guests that we did not lie in our services! Isn't it interesting to know that this is how we are training our "young champions?" We start them off by assuring them that they can't count on the Holy Spirit to do His job, so we use dishonesty and pressure to take His place. Isn't that what it really amounts to?

I recently attended the services of an evangelist who once again assured the people the he would not come down and embarrass or approach anyone during the invitation time. Using this tactic to get them to "drop their guard" and have them feel like they are "safe" to be honest, he then encouraged anyone in the auditorium who had a burden for someone else in the auditorium, to approach them and assure them that they were willing to go to the altar with them. So much for implying that they would not be approached! And, yes, during that invitation, a lost person left the auditorium crying and very upset. After being deceived that way – I don't blame her!

And while we're on the subject of pressure, do you really think that the Apostles sang 56 stanzas of "Just as I Am?" You would get rid of this attitude that "they are going to get away and go to hell," if you would come back to putting some confidence in the Holy Spirit! If you would learn to trust Him to do what His job is, we would all get to the Sunday buffet a little earlier! Pressure is not good in an invitation; whether it be applied to the lost or to the saved! A guest pastor speaking in a church where I was present at the revival services, started into the invitation time by saying, "I'm not inviting you to come to the altar, I'm telling you to come to the altar," to which I responded by walking out the door! Where do we come off taking the place of the Holy Spirit, whether it's with the saved or the lost? I've witnessed so many "forced invitations" since I've been saved, that I begin to wonder if we Baptists believe there is a Holy Ghost anymore! You would do well to remember that you are only the messenger boy, and the job of conviction does not belong to you!

# CHAPTER 12

# MISINTERPRETATION OF THE SOWER

There are those who justify all their "missing converts" with the parable of the Sower. "Keep in mind," say they, "that Jesus taught that only one out of four would make it anyway." Of course Jesus didn't teach that, but when you're grasping for straws to justify your mishandling of people's souls, I guess one misinterpretation is as good as another! Neither the group on "stony places" nor the group among "thorns" suggests in any way that they didn't even make it to church. To the contrary, Matthew 13:21 says that they **"...dureth for a while..."** That's not quite the same as never showing up for the first church service! Similarly, Mark 4:17 reads, **"...endure but for a time..."** while verse 19 says, **"...and it becometh unfruitful."** This is not the language of someone who prayed a prayer after someone on a street corner somewhere, and never darkened the door of the church! Perhaps the language of Luke 8:13 will make it clearer to you, "They on the rock are they, which, when they hear, receive the word with joy; and these have no root, which for a while believe, and in time of temptation fall away."

Friend, you will never use the parable of the Sower to justify three out of four of your "converts" never seeing the church house, because that is not what the Scripture teaches at all. To the contrary, it seems to indicate that three out of four of the groups will make it to church, but only one group bears fruit! Besides, to say that these two groups represent your false professions, is to deny that these two groups are actually in the midst of our congregations now! There is not a pastor reading this book that could not testify to the fact that they have had countless numbers of church folks who were knocked off track through temptations and trials! Likewise in all our pastorates, we have witnessed good folks who have been fruitless due to the lust of the things of this world. Each of these two groups, fruitless - yes; but never darkening the door of the church - no! You're going to have to come up with a better explanation of your 738 saved and 25 baptized!

## CHAPTER 13

## "YOU CAN WIN PEOPLE ANYWHERE!"

We all have had the dubious privilege of hearing some great soul-winning lecture where we were put on a guilt trip for not having throngs of people saved in our respective churches. The theme is usually, you are lazy, or you lack a burden, or you are not "out in the trenches," or you are not doing it their way, etc. etc. etc. "You can win people everywhere!" is the battle cry. "It's the same everywhere!" echoes another. "The gospel still works everywhere; the problem, is that you are not working it!" declares another. "One, two, three, pray after me," says the master manipulator. Their remarks are well meaning, if they are intending to get people to be a witness, but, some of the afore-mentioned remarks are contradicted in the Bible!

Of course, we all know that Noah preached for 120 years without a convert! He obviously missed the lecture, "You can win people anywhere!" But for those of our readers who feel as though that doesn't count because it is Old Testament, let's view some New Testament passages that obviously missed the lecture also.

Jesus names a few cities where it seems as though "it couldn't be done" regardless of what our soul-winning friends say. Let's begin at Matthew 11:20-23. **"Then began he to upbraid the cities wherein most of his mighty works were done, because they repented not: Woe**

**unto thee, Chorazin! woe unto thee, Bethsaida! for if the mighty works, which were done in you, had been done in Tyre and Sidon, they would have repented long ago in sackcloth and ashes. But I say unto you, It shall be more tolerable for Tyre and Sidon at the day of judgment, than for you. And thou, Capernaum, which art exalted unto heaven, shalt be brought down to hell: for if the mighty works, which have been done in thee, had been done in Sodom, it would have remained until this day."** You wouldn't want to tell Jesus that it will work "anywhere" would you?

An account is given in Luke 9:53 and 54, where two of His apostles were so upset that you couldn't "win people to Jesus anywhere" that they requested that He let them call fire down from heaven and burn them up. **"And they did not receive him, because his face was as though he would go to Jerusalem. And when his disciples James and John saw this, they said, Lord, wilt thou that we command fire to come down from heaven, and consume them, even as Elias did?"** Some of the statements of our "Super Soul-winners" don't seem to line up with the experiences of Jesus Himself! The difference lies in what they really mean by "You can win people anywhere." They mean that you can impart intellectual knowledge, or that you can manipulate them in a prayer, or control their will – but none of these things will bring an individual to the new birth!!

Rather than teach His disciples that "you can win people anywhere," He taught them the exact opposite! Ponder His teaching Matthew 10:14. **"And whosoever shall not receive you, nor hear your words, when ye depart out of that house or city, shake off the dust from your feet."** Consider Luke 9:5. **"And whosoever will not receive you, when ye go out of that city, shake off the very dust from your feet for a testimony against them."** If you can "win people anywhere" then why did Jesus tell His disciples that there would be entire cities that would not give ear to the gospel? Some of us prefer Jesus' course over your course!

The most refreshing missionary that I have hear in a long time, gave his update to our church recently. He has been in Poland for 14 years and to date knows of only 5 people who have been saved under his ministry. Just like at Pentecost, he only counts the ones who have been saved, baptized, and are in the church. Most of our "one, two, three, pray after me" fellows, would have dropped his support a long time ago! Myself, I would drop the guy with 738 saved and 25 baptized, and shift his support to the fellow from Poland!

## CHAPTER 14

## GO ALL THE WAY!

Although some of the information in this chapter may seem repetitious, we are approaching bad practices from a different angle. Many who teach their "soul-winning courses" will insist that you always go for the "gold ring on the merry-go-round" every single time that you have an encounter. Even though that sounds like you are being about the Master's business, I'll show you momentarily that even "The Master" didn't practice such an endeavor! As stated in a previous chapter, this very thought goes contrary to the teaching of planting and watering in a genuine witness encounter! And, it switches it from God's farming illustration to retail sales.

Watch "The Master" of soul-winning at work with Nicodemus, in John chapter three. He gave him the life changing message, let him ask Him questions, with no pressure applied, and then let him walk away lost! I'm sure that He would have received great criticism from our "great soul-winners" of today! Jesus, however, incorporated a unique factor that is missing today – it's called the work of the Holy Ghost! Somewhere between John chapter three and chapter nineteen Nicodemus got saved. You and I don't know where, but as far as the scripture record indicates, he never had another physical encounter with Jesus. What it amounts to brethren is that the second Person of the Godhead trusted the third

Person of the Godhead to do His designated work. I suggest that you and I do likewise!

Another encounter with The Master was the scribe in Mark chapter twelve. Reading in verse 34, "And when Jesus saw that he answered discreetly, he said unto him, Thou art not far from the kingdom of God. And no man after that durst ask him any question." Boy would Brother So-n-So be upset with Jesus if He were his student! You see, "not far" still meant not ready to Jesus! Today, someone would have "led" that scribe in prayer and put a notch on their soul-winning gun." Can we not trust that when people are "not far from the kingdom" that The Holy Ghost will help them to find their way?

Then there was the Apostle Paul with King Agrippa in Acts chapter twenty-six. He stated the message, assured him that he desired that he would get saved, and then stopped short of "leading him in a prayer." Paul did not "go all the way," because he had enough spiritual discernment to understand that Agrippa was not willing to surrender his will in this matter of salvation. We have all but forgotten that man has been made a free will creature, and that he must make the decision, under the convicting power of the Holy Ghost of God, to surrender that will to the Saviour! Most of our brethren operate under the assumption that they must "break that will" in order to get a convert saved. That's the reason for all the pressure and psychology in most soul-winning courses and literatures!

So, how do we correct this "go all the way" practice? The answer is very simple – Never go any farther than the recipient wants to go! When you sense reluctance – back off! The Nicodemus's of life will always show up in the later chapters! "But," you say, "what about the king Agrippas?" I believe that the Apostle Paul would rather be able to say at the Judgment seat of Christ, that his hands were free from Agrippa's blood, than to be told that he "pushed him into hell" with a false profession! "But," you say, "the false profession was Agrippa's fault and not Paul's," to which I would say that, "if you handled that soul contrary to scriptural teaching – the false profession is your responsibility!"

# CHAPTER 15

# DON'T TRUST THE HOLY GHOST

I almost feel blasphemous even writing this chapter title, but I really feel as though this is our current position, as a whole, in the Independent Baptist movement. We are indicating this in our invitation services, in our personal encounters with the lost, and in our general unwillingness to let Him do His work. I don't know what all of the reasons are, but I do know that much of it amounts to you and I wanting to "grab the glory!" For, you see, the Nicodemus's are not those that you can sit around at your fellowship meetings and brag about to the brethren! When you and I don't "force a prayer" on someone during an encounter, we have no way of knowing when the Holy Spirit completes His work in their hearts, so we can't grab the glory. Have you ever noticed that preachers don't usually brag about the seeding or watering (which is their part of the process) but rather "the increase" which is God's! Have you ever seen them pat one another on the back because they made 25 good visits last week? Or, what kind of notoriety do they give one another for the number of people they witnessed to last year?

In my earlier pastor years, I had a well-known evangelist preach revival services for me. When I took note that he had the habit of coming down from the pulpit during his invitation, and confronting those who had "raised their hands for prayer," I instructed him not to do that anymore. I was surprised at his response, when he suggested to me that those folks would go to hell if they left the services without being approached (pressured), and it would be all my fault! I asked him if the Holy Ghost was confined to his invitation, or if He simply didn't know where they lived! Needless to say, he wasn't back for any more meetings, by mutual consent! When we were celebrating heaven-sent revival in our churches, nobody had to drag people down the aisle - they ran down on their own! That's back when we trusted the Holy Ghost to do His work! Let's get back to the old paths on this subject, and let Him work on people, instead of us trying to take His place!

## CHAPTER 16

## GASHMU SAITH IT!

Remember back in Nehemiah chapter six, when Sanballat and Tobiah, the enemies of the Jews, tried to get Nehemiah to meet with them so that they could stop the building of the walls in Jerusalem? When he refused, they then threatened to write to the King and tell him that Nehemiah was planning to make himself a king and rebel against Artaxerxes. As an extra measure to make this lie believable, they stated that they were going to tell King Artaxerxes that Gashmu saith it was so. You'll find this in Nehemiah 6:6, **"Wherein was written, It is reported among the heathen, and Gashmu saith it, that thou and the Jews think to rebel: for which cause thou buildest the wall, that thou mayest be their king, according to these words."** Whoever this Gashmu character was, his name must have been much set by with the king. They felt as though their lie would be stronger and have a better chance of being believed, if they were to attach Gashmu's name to it.

It seems as though this has become the pattern for the Independent Baptist movement! As long as you can attach Brother So-n-So's name to an unscriptural practice, it will place more credence to a lie! My friend, all the Gashmus in the world cannot change God's prescribed method of working with an individual's soul, nor does it turn a lie into the truth! Anyone who denies the need for conviction and repentance in a soul-winning experience is a liar! Anyone who instructs you to use a vehicle other than the one that has been assigned to you (see chapter one), is guilty of misrepresenting God's plan! Anyone who indicates that your reward is based upon how many people you "lead to Christ" has misled you! The Gashmus of this world march on, but that doesn't change a lie into the truth!

Perhaps our real need is to stop reading the material of the Gashmus and spend a little more time in God's Word! Most of our soul-winning practices line up with the Gashmus and not with the Bible, which helps me to understand why we are claiming so many conversions and so few additions! If you add up the number of professions that some of our pastor friends have each year, and multiply it by the number of years they have been in that church, it would in some cases exceed the number of people that live in their area! Some of the missionary letters that I have read lately, brings me to the conclusion that we will be able to call all of the missionaries home within the next ten years, because the entire population of that country will then be saved. No beloved, improper practices are lining people up at the gates of hell today, thinking they are saved, because some "soul-winner" told them they were. You have a choice. Listen to what Gashmu saith – or what the Bible saith!

# CHAPTER 17

# BELIEVING IN VAIN

Just as repentance was injected at the cross, by way of the penitent thief, so also is the false profession in the midst of the description of the gospel. Let's note it in 1 Corinthians 15:1-4. **"Moreover, brethren, I declare unto you to gospel which I preached unto you, which also ye have received, and wherein ye stand; By which also ye are saved, if ye keep in memory what I preached unto you, unless ye have believed in vain. For I delivered unto you first of all that which I also received, how that Christ died for our sins according to the scriptures; And that he was buried, and that he rose again the third day according to the scriptures:"** The word "vain" gives the idea of idly, without reason or effect. You know, like the tens of thousands of people whose "salvation" seems to have no effect on the way they live, after they make that "profession!"

They arrive at a salvation that has no effect on their (vain) lives, because they have been presented with a salvation that would not affect their lives! When is the last time you informed a convert that the decision you were asking them to make would affect their life and living for the rest of their pilgrim journey? Are you afraid that if you take the time to explain "the new creature concept" of 2 Corinthians 5:17 that you will have one less souls to add to your report? One of the phrases folks have heard me say most over the years goes something like this, "If Christ is not going to change your life, what do you need Him for anyway?" What they hear soul-winners say the most today goes something like this, "You don't have to do a thing to get saved right now." As far as works verses grace is concerned, that is true, but the remark can be, and is, very misleading. They do have to repent you know! Repentance is a heart attitude more than an act of works! We almost approach this "you don't have to do a thing to get saved right now" issue, as if everything will go on as "business as usual," from the time they get saved to the end of their lives!

Then there is the matter of 2 Corinthians 7:10, **"For godly sorrow worketh repentance to salvation not to be repented of: but the sorrow of the world worketh death."** Let me paraphrase that without doing any injustice to the teaching, "Sorrow that is of God will work a genuine repentance leading to true salvation that a person will not turn back from, but worldly sorrow on the other hand will accomplish nothing." Sounds like a pretty good distinction between a false profession of faith and a true profession of faith! How do you accomplish "godly sorrow" as opposed to "the sorrow of the world?" God, the Holy Spirit, accomplishes godly sorrow, and when you and I leave Him out, we arrive at the sorrow of the world! Let the One Who is not of this world work out the sorrow, and you won't have to worry about arriving at worldly sorrow! I'll bet you get tired of me going down that same road.

Remembering that "vain" means, idly, without reason or effect, how is it that I can avoid having people "believe in vain?" Simply put, if you try to do the repenting, it will have no effect toward a true conversion resulting in a changed life. Likewise, if you try to do the convicting, it will be of no effect to the recipient! You may get him or her to pray a prayer, but that prayer will be "without effect," and the vain emptiness of their lives will be quite evident.

Where is our remaining fruit?

**"Ye have not chosen me, but I have chosen you, and ordained you, that ye should go and bring forth fruit, and that your fruit should remain: that whatsoever ye shall ask of the Father in my name, he may give it you."**

## ABOUT THE AUTHOR

Brother Bob brings to the table over 45 years of Bible study, besides his BA in Pastoral Theology. He has accumulated 13 yea.rs at the pastorate, and over 30 years as an evangelist and missionary. His accomplishments include the founding of one church and author of several booklets. He preached several radio broadcast, mission conferences, and pastor's conferences. The father of 4 children, 10 grandchildren, and 2 great grandchildren, he believes very strongly in the Biblical structure of the home. He currently occupies the position of director, at the The Desert Place Haven of Rest, an independent Baptist pastors retreat. The location of this Home Missions Project is nestled in the foothills of the beautiful Smoky Mountains. Bro Bob founded this project, and has been with it since its conception in 1993.

Brother Creel's prayer card is on the next page.

# THE DESERT PLACE HAVEN OF REST

"And he said unto them, Come ye yourselves apart into a desert place, and rest a while: for there were many coming and going, and they had no leisure so much as to eat." Mark.6:31

## INFORMATION:

This beautiful retreat is nestled in the foothills of the Great Smoky Mountains, and available at no cost to Independent Baptist Pastors and their Families who meet the necessary doctrinal criterion.

Please help us in prayer and financial support, that these spiritual warriors will have the necessary R & R needed in these last critical days.

The Desert Place Haven Of Rest
P.O. Box 4548
Sevierville, TN 37864
865-712-4537

www.ingramcontent.com/pod-product-compliance
Lightning Source LLC
La Vergne TN
LVHW050942080826
845145LV00004B/1380

* 9 7 8 1 7 3 5 6 7 2 3 9 7 *